W9-ASK-669

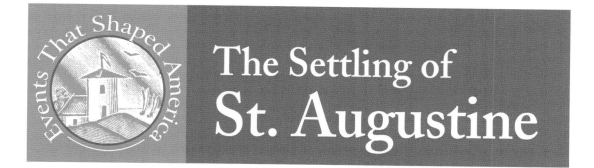

The Settling of
St. Augustine

Sabrina Crewe and Janet Riehecky

Gareth Stevens Publishing
A WORLD ALMANAC EDUCATION GROUP COMPANY

Please visit our web site at: www.garethstevens.com
For a free color catalog describing Gareth Stevens Publishing's list of high-quality
books and multimedia programs, call 1-800-542-2595 (USA) or 1-800-387-3178
(Canada). Gareth Stevens Publishing's fax: (414) 332-3567.

Library of Congress Cataloging-in-Publication Data

Crewe, Sabrina.
    The settling of St. Augustine / by Sabrina Crewe and Janet Riehecky.
      p. cm. — (Events that shaped America)
    Includes bibliographical references and index.
    ISBN 0-8368-3395-3 (lib. bdg.)
    1. Saint Augustine (Fla.)—History—Juvenile literature. 2. Spaniards—Florida—Saint
Augustine—History—Juvenile literature. 3. Timucua Indians—Florida—Saint Augustine—
History—Juvenile literature. 4. Florida—History—To 1821—Juvenile literature. [1. Saint
Augustine (Fla.)—History. 2. Timucua Indians. 3. Indians of North America—Florida.]
I. Title: Settling of Saint Augustine. II. Riehecky, Janet, 1953- . III. Title. IV. Series.
F319.S2C74 2003
975.9'18—dc21
                        2002030992

First published in 2003 by
Gareth Stevens Publishing
A World Almanac Education Group Company
330 West Olive Street, Suite 100
Milwaukee, WI 53212 USA

Produced by Discovery Books
Editor: Sabrina Crewe
Designer and page production: Sabine Beaupré
Photo researcher: Sabrina Crewe
Maps and diagrams: Stefan Chabluk
Gareth Stevens editorial direction: Mark J. Sachner
Gareth Stevens art direction: Tammy Gruenewald
Gareth Stevens production: Jessica Yanke

Photo credits: Corbis: pp. 4, 6, 12, 13, 14, 16, 18, 19, 20, 22 (top), 25, 26, 27;
The Granger Collection: cover, p. 11; North Wind Picture Archives: pp. 5, 7,
8, 9, 10, 15, 21, 24, 22 (bottom).

Printed in the United States of America

1 2 3 4 5 6 7 8 9 07 06 05 04 03

Contents

Introduction

Ready to Sail

"Pedro Menéndez obliges himself that within the coming month of May, he will have ready and equipped to sail [ten ships] loaded with supplies and put in condition for war. . . . He will carry five hundred men, one hundred farmers, one hundred sailors and the rest men and officers of sea and war, and among these there will be at least two clerics and other persons, skilled in stonecutting, carpentry, and **farriers**, blacksmiths and surgeons."

Agreement between Spanish Council and Pedro Menéndez de Avilés, signed by King Philip II, March 20, 1565

A Spanish Settlement

In 1565, King Philip II of Spain signed an agreement with a sailor and explorer named Pedro Menéndez de Avilés. The agreement said that Menéndez would found a settlement in an area of North America that is now the state of Florida.

Spain already had large, flourishing **colonies** in Central and South America and on islands in the Caribbean Sea, but it had yet to establish any north of Mexico. King Philip was hopeful that the Florida region would produce valuable **natural resources**, as other colonies had done.

This is the city of St. Augustine today. In the 1500s, St. Augustine struggled to survive, but it has grown into a prosperous city.

Before the Spanish arrived, Florida was a heavily forested region with a traditional society that had existed for thousands of years. This is a replica of a shelter built by the Timucuan people who inhabited the St. Augustine area long ago.

In September 1565, Menéndez landed in Florida near the Native American village of Seloy. There, his men built a settlement that was named St. Augustine.

The Colony Survives

The Spanish **colonists** in St. Augustine struggled, but they survived. St. Augustine became an important port for Spanish ships carrying goods from other colonies. The city established courts of law, businesses, and an education system many years before any British colonies in North America. Today, St. Augustine is the oldest existing European settlement in the United States.

Everything Changes

Settlement by Europeans, starting with St. Augustine, caused everything to change. The way of life in North America had been about the same for thousands of years. The arrival of the Europeans, however, meant the end of traditional ways of life. Even the environment changed. New species of plants and animals were brought from Europe. Across the continent, forests were cut down. Within a short space of time, millions of people died and Native American societies were destroyed.

Chapter One

Before the Europeans

The People of Florida

Native Americans lived in Florida for thousands of years before Europeans came to North America. In the early 1500s, the people who lived near present-day St. Augustine called themselves the Saturiba. Europeans, however, called them Timucuan Indians, which was their name for all Native groups in northern Florida.

The Village

Timucuan villages were organized into groups. Each group was a chiefdom and was ruled by a great chief. The number of villages in a chiefdom could be anything from two to forty or more. Each Timucuan village, which could consist of up to two hundred houses, had its own chief and council. In

the center of each village stood the council house, which was larger than the other houses. The chief lived in the council house, and it was also used for meetings.

Ordinary houses in Timucuan villages were round or oval, about 20 or 25 feet (6 to 7.6 meters) across, and made of **saplings** stuck into the ground. The saplings were bent inward to form a domed roof. People wove plants around the saplings to make walls, and the walls and roof were then covered with **thatch**. There were two holes, one for a door and the other to let out smoke through the roof.

These Florida men are training for various sports. Some are running races and others are competing with bows and arrows. One group plays a game in which a ball is thrown up at a square on a post, like basketball without the basket.

The Ais, Tequesta, and Calusa lived in southern Florida. To the north, in what are now eastern Florida and southern Georgia, were the Apalache and Guale peoples.

What They Wore

Because of the warm climate in Florida, Timucuans wore little clothing, usually just a loincloth or skirt made of deerskin. Both men and women wore their hair long, but men tied theirs up on top of their heads. If a warrior died, his widow cut off her hair and left it on his grave. She could not remarry until her short hair grew back to shoulder length.

Florida people wore bird feathers and necklaces of shells, pearls, or fish teeth. Men also wore earrings and plates of gold, silver, or brass on their legs. Both men and women decorated their bodies with paint for ceremonies.

In Florida, the Native people were farmers. The men are preparing the ground while a woman drills holes for corn seed. Another woman sows the seed.

Farmers and Hunters

Timucuan people spent much of their time in getting food. The men hunted animals, such as deer, alligator, and rabbits, and they caught fish. Both men and women farmed: men prepared the ground and women did the planting. Corn was their most important crop, but they also planted beans, squash, and pumpkins. In addition, women and children gathered wild berries, nuts, oysters, clams, and birds' eggs.

Spiritual Ceremonies

Timucuans gave honor to the Sun as the source of life. Their priest led ceremonies of worship before hunting trips or on other significant occasions. One of the most important ceremonies was to welcome spring. The body of a stag, with the horns still on, was stuffed with herbs. It was then hung on a high tree, facing east, as an offering to the Sun.

European Contact

There were maybe 200,000 Timucuan people in Florida before the Spanish settlers arrived in the 1500s. The Spanish and other Europeans, however, brought diseases to which Native people had never been exposed. **Epidemics** raged through Florida, killing whole villages. Those who resisted Spanish rule were often sold as slaves or killed. Most of the Timucuan population died out soon after the first contact with Europeans. By the end of the 1700s, there were no Timucuans left at all.

Hunting Deer

"The Indians, when hunting deer, . . . fitted the skins of the largest deer that they have been able to catch over their bodies so that the deer's head covered their own and they were able to look through the eye holes as if it were a mask. . . . There were a lot of deer in that region so they were easily able to shoot them with their bows and arrows. . . . They were able to remove the deer skin and prepare it without any metal knife, just shells, with such skill that I doubt there was anyone in the whole of Europe who could do it better."

From the journal of French artist Jacques Le Moyne, 1564

Chapter Two

The Spanish Come to Florida

Attempts at Colonization

In the early 1500s, Florida was claimed by the Spanish **Empire**. It was never the most important part of the empire, but Spain tried to explore and colonize the area.

The Spanish Empire

The Spanish Empire in the Americas began in the islands of the Caribbean and in Mexico. This happened in the early 1500s, when the Spanish arrived in search of riches, especially gold. Spain had soon claimed great chunks of the Caribbean as well as Mexico and parts of Central and South America. The Spanish didn't care that there were already people living in these places. In fact, they used the local people as slave labor so that they could acquire wealth for themselves. Soon, ships laden with gold, silver, and other natural resources were traveling back to Spain.

Havana on the island of Cuba was a busy port and center for Spanish trade in the Caribbean.

Spain's first colonies failed mostly because of the Spanish attitude. The Spaniards thought Native people were savages and that their own way of doing things was superior. Because of this, the Spanish didn't adapt very well to life in Florida. The settlers didn't have the skills to hunt, fish, or grow their own food, and they weren't willing to learn from local people.

Taking Slaves

Even though they didn't manage to settle, Spanish people often landed on the coast of Florida to capture Native people to sell as slaves. Sometimes they traded goods, but usually they just took what they wanted by force. Not surprisingly, the people of Florida fought back, attacking Spanish soldiers and explorers who landed in their country. Sometimes they told the Spanish there was gold to the north or west just to get rid of them. Until the 1560s, one way or another, the people of Florida managed to keep most invaders out.

Hernando de Soto, shown here on horseback, came to Florida to find gold in 1639. His soldiers captured and killed many Native people and spread European diseases among the villages.

The Naming of Florida

Juan Ponce de León, Spanish governor of the Caribbean island of Puerto Rico, heard stories of an island of great wealth called Bimini, north of Cuba. On March 3, 1513, he set sail from Puerto Rico to look for Bimini. On Easter Sunday, March 27, lookouts sighted land. Because of the day, Ponce de León named the place he saw *Pascua Florida*, Spanish for "flowery Easter." Ponce de León hadn't found an island, as he thought. What he had seen was the North American coastline.

Chapter Three

Founding the Settlement

Taking the Land

"He [will go] . . . to the Coast of Florida. . . . If there are on the said coast or land some . . . settlers or any other peoples not subject to His Majesty, arrange to throw them out by the best means possible, which seem best to him. Take the land of the said Florida for His Majesty and in his royal name, attempting to bring its natives to the obedience of His Majesty. . . ."

Agreement between Spanish Council and Pedro Menéndez de Avilés, signed by King Philip II, March 20, 1565

In March 1565, after the other Spanish colonies in Florida had all failed, King Philip II of Spain asked one of his naval officers, Pedro Menéndez de Avilés, to try again. The king appointed Menéndez as governor of Florida. Menéndez began preparations to leave for Florida and establish a new settlement.

Pedro Menéndez (1519–1574)

Pedro Menéndez was born in Avilés in Spain. As a young man, he became an officer in the Spanish navy. He rose to the rank of admiral and became famous fighting pirates. Appointed as governor of Florida, Menéndez set up his colonial capital in St. Augustine. While he was governor, Menéndez continued to explore, found new settlements, and fight other European nations on Spain's behalf. In 1574, he was in Spain assembling a **fleet** of ships when he developed a fever and died.

A huge steel cross, 208 feet (63 m) high, towers over St. Augustine Bay. It marks the place where the first religious service was held when the Spanish landed in 1565.

Traveling to Florida

Near the beginning of July 1565, Menéndez set sail from Spain. He started out with nineteen ships, but most of them met storms while crossing the Atlantic Ocean. Only five ships eventually made their way to Florida. They carried about 500 soldiers, 200 sailors, and 100 others, including women, children, and craftspeople.

Menéndez found a good harbor near the site of the Timucuan village of Seloy. The fact that the place already had a name and people living there didn't matter to Menéndez. He renamed the place St. Augustine after the Catholic saint who was honored on August 28. This was the day that the expedition had first spotted the Florida coast.

The French Arrive First

While Menéndez was preparing to go to Florida and found a settlement, King Philip learned that France, Spain's enemy, had already sent an expedition to do the same thing! King Philip told Menéndez to destroy the French colony on arrival. Spain did not want the French establishing a base from which to attack Spanish ships. Also, the

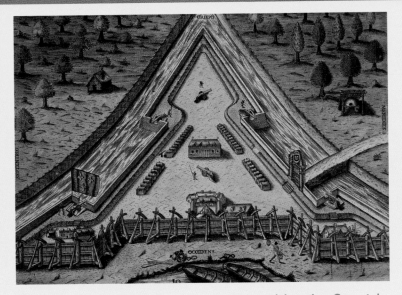

Fort Caroline before it was captured by the Spanish.

French settlers were Protestants. The Spanish were Catholics and they hated Protestants. They persecuted Protestants in their own country and certainly didn't want them settling anywhere in the Spanish Empire.

The French colonists landed in 1564 and built Fort Caroline about 45 miles (72 kilometers) north of where St. Augustine would be. Fort Caroline was home to about three hundred people.

On September 20, 1865, Menéndez and his soldiers captured the French fort. They executed most of the settlers and took a few as prisoners. Menéndez renamed Fort Caroline as San Mateo and installed some soldiers there.

A Colony on Timucuan Land

Menéndez told his men to take over Seloy and make a fort out of the council house. Nobody is sure if Seloy's residents stayed in the village or moved away. The Timucuans were friendly to the new arrivals, however. They traded food and furs for metal tools and other European goods.

14

The good relations didn't last. As usual, the Spanish soldiers showed little respect and simply took by force whatever they wanted. Some Timucuans remained friendly, but others began attacking any Spaniard who left the fort.

Starvation

When St. Augustine started running out of food in the fall of 1565, Menéndez took some of his soldiers and sailed to Havana, Cuba. From there, he sent supplies back to Florida. Even so, people in St. Augustine began to starve during the winter of 1565–66. Several hundred soldiers simply deserted the town. They either joined the Timucuans or sailed to the Caribbean. Other colonists got sick. In all, St. Augustine lost almost half its original settlers that first winter.

Colonists start laying out the town at St. Augustine. In the background, a group clusters around the priest for religious services.

Timucuan attacks were often successful in spite of the fact that soldiers had guns that were much more powerful than the Native bows and arrows. The Native men were very skilled with their weapons and were more familiar with the land.

Rebuilding

In May 1566, the Timucuan chiefdoms declared war on the Spanish. They burned down the fort in St. Augustine. Menéndez returned to restore order and rebuild the fort, this time on Anastasia Island across the bay. He arranged for regular supplies from Cuba. In early summer of 1566, a fleet of ships from Spain arrived, bringing more than a thousand new soldiers. St. Augustine became more secure, and the settlers continued to build their town.

The Plan

"He shall build and populate [within] three years two or three towns in the places and ports which seem to him the best. . . . He shall attempt to place, within the said three years, five hundred slaves for his service and for that of the people, in order that the towns might be built with more facility and the land might be cultivated. . . ."

Agreement between Spanish Council and Pedro Menéndez de Avilés, signed by King Philip II, March 20, 1565

New Colonists

The Timucuans continued their attacks on the colony at St. Augustine, however. They also attacked other Spanish settlements founded by Menéndez over the next few years.

By summer of 1568, San Mateo was destroyed and the colonists at St. Augustine were in bad shape. In 1569, Menéndez brought in eighty new colonists who had better skills for settling the land than his soldiers did. These new settlers quickly started improving the colony. They built houses, planted crops, tended livestock, and built up trade.

The settlement was moved back to the mainland in 1572, after six years on Anastasia Island. By the mid-1570s, pig farms and cornfields had been established. Somehow, St. Augustine and one other settlement, Santa Elena, struggled along until Pedro Menéndez died in 1574.

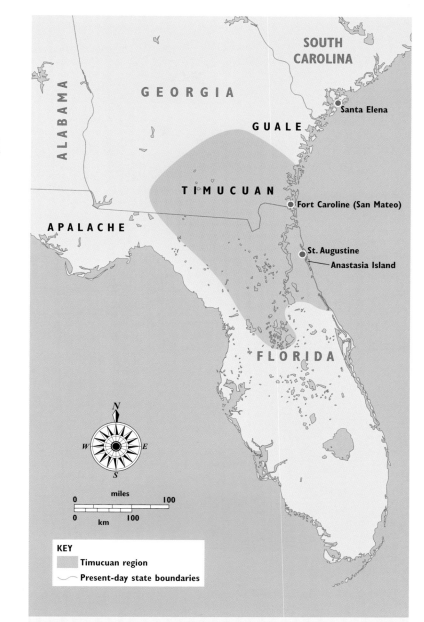

This map shows the areas where the Timucuan people and their Guale and Apalache neighbors lived before the Spanish came. It also shows the Spanish settlements of San Mateo (previously Fort Caroline), St. Augustine, and Santa Elena.

Chapter Four

Life in St. Augustine

Rich Lands

"What I say to Your Majesty about this land of which all the world says ill, is that it is a marvel of good, because there are most rich lands for tillage and stock-farms, powerful rivers of sweet water, great fertile plains and mountains."

Colonist Bartolomé Martínez, in a letter to King Philip II, February 17, 1577

Peace with the Timucuans

In 1576, Santa Elena was attacked by Native people and destroyed. The people fled to St. Augustine, but Native people attacked there, too, and destroyed the houses. About 180 survivors took refuge in the fort.

After this, Spain appointed Pedro Menéndez Marquez, a nephew of the first Pedro Menéndez, as Florida's new governor. He made peace with the Timucuans, and things got a little better. Until 1698, however, St. Augustine was Spain's only settlement in Florida apart from the **missions**.

Over the years, as one disaster after another struck St. Augustine, its houses were built and rebuilt. None of the first houses still exists. These dwellings in the city are of a type built by the Spanish in the 1600s.

The People of St. Augustine

By 1580, St. Augustine had grown again, and it had 275 colonists. Of these, 110 were soldiers, 20 were seamen, and 100 were women and children. The remaining 45 were priests, town officials, and craftsmen.

Because there were so few Spanish women, many men had Timucuan wives. In 1580, about one-fourth of the households had a Native female as a member. Over the next few years, African slaves and convicts from Spain would also join the population.

A Spanish Town

In 1580, St. Augustine had a church and several shops. About a hundred new houses had been built since the town was destroyed in 1576. St. Augustine was laid out like a Spanish town, with a central square surrounded by small houses along narrow streets.

Most men in St. Augustine were soldiers stationed at the fort. These men are dressed as Spanish soldiers in a show for visitors to St. Augustine's ancient fort.

This room is in a reconstructed house in St. Augustine's Spanish Quarter. It shows visitors what living quarters were like in the colony in the early 1700s.

Usually, the houses contained two rooms and sat on plots of land 44 feet by 88 feet (13.4 m by 26.8 m). They were half-timbered, which means they had wooden frames covered with mud or clay. Their roofs were thatched. Kitchens were always in separate buildings to reduce smells, heat, and fire risk in the main house. Most houses had a courtyard or garden in the back, and some had a stable.

Every house had its own well to supply water. The colonists also collected water in large clay jars called *tinajones*. These huge vessels were placed under the eaves of a house to catch the rainwater and buried partly underground to keep the water cool.

Barely Surviving

". . . in all this district there has been sown corn, beans, and squash, and other fruits and legumes, and [even though] it is of great help for the sustenance of the people who live and serve His Majesty here, it is not sufficient to be able to sustain themselves without the salary and ration that they have, and even with this they survive only frugally."

Report by royal official Alonso de las Alas, September 15, 1602

Food in St. Augustine

For most people in St. Augustine, getting enough food to survive was a struggle. Colonists traded with the Timucuans for food and raised some of their own. Families were assigned garden plots outside the town, where they grew corn and vegetables. They planted fruit trees, usually oranges or figs, in their yards. Most people lived on corn, beans, pumpkin, oranges, peaches, figs, and fish. If they could get meat, it was usually poultry, raccoons, opossums, and deer. Richer people could also buy the meat of cattle and pigs raised in the colony.

Daily Life

The Catholic religion was an important part of daily life in St. Augustine, and everyone attended church. Priests held daily services and also established the first public schools in North America.

For most colonists, the day was devoted to chores. Crops were planted and tended, meals were cooked, and clothes were mended and washed.

St. Augustine settlers relied on Timucuans for much of their food. This group is bringing harvested food to a large storehouse for winter supplies.

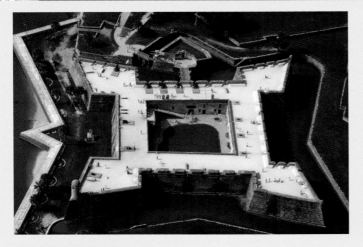

It took twenty-three years to build St. Augustine's stone fort, the Castillo de San Marcos, which was begun in 1671. The Castillo was built of *coquina*, a yellow stone formed from layers of seashells. Blocks of coquina were held together with a paste, made from oyster shells, that hardened when it dried.

The Castillo de San Marcos is a square structure that has **bastions** protruding from each corner. Cannons and **mortars** are perched around the fort. The walls are about 20 feet (6 m) high, and a deep **moat** surrounds the whole building. The only entrance is a narrow drawbridge over the moat on the side of the fort facing the town.

Above: An aerial view of the Castillo de San Marcos.

Left: A bronze mortar added to the fort in 1724.

Spoiling the Town

"The 28. of May early in the morning we [saw] Saynt Augustine in Florida, in 36. degrees of latitude, wher some small Spanish **Garrison** was planted, of some 150 men, or thereabouts: Here we spent two dayes in taking the fort and spoiling the Town, and so departed agayn . . ."

From the log of Sir Francis Drake, 1586

Attacks

St. Augustine was still mostly a military town, dominated by its fort. Soldiers on guard duty took six-hour watches, looking out for **privateers**. These were English, Dutch, or French adventurers encouraged by their governments to attack Spanish ships carrying goods from the colonies back to Europe.

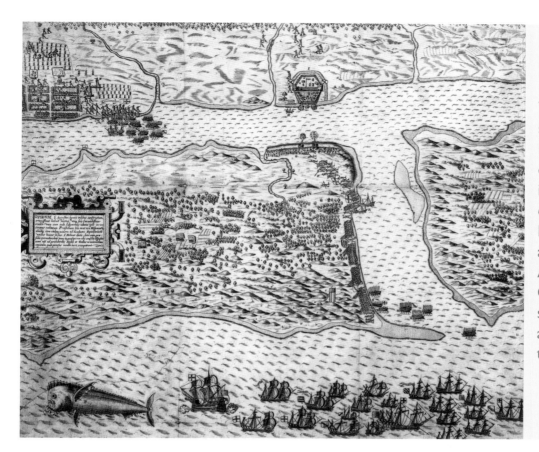

This picture shows Francis Drake's attack on St. Augustine in 1586. In the center, the British are firing at the fort from Anastasia Island. On the left, soldiers are attacking the town.

Privateers also attacked Spanish settlements, and St. Augustine was attacked several times. The worst attack was in June 1586. A fleet of forty-two ships under the command of English adventurer Francis Drake sailed into the harbor. When the colonists fled, the English looted the city and then burned all the houses.

Natural Disasters

The Spanish soon rebuilt their town, but it didn't last long. In 1599, another fire swept through St. Augustine, burning down part of the town. Then a hurricane caused the sea to rise, which flooded what was left. So the Spanish rebuilt yet again!

Rebuilding the City
"With the cutting down of the timber it has done away with the vast quantities of mosquitoes and has helped to improve the city, as one sees on all sides houses in course of construction."

St. Augustine colonist Redondo Villegas, letter to King Philip III of Spain, April 18, 1600

Chapter Five

The Missions

A Duty to Convert

While all this building and rebuilding of St. Augustine was going on, what happened to the Native people? The Spanish believed it was their duty to **convert** Native people to Catholicism. It also was a good way to gain control over them and exploit their labor.

St. Augustine's cathedral is built in the Spanish mission style. High up under the church bells is a statue of St. Augustine himself.

Being a Convert

When Native people were **baptized**, they were given Spanish names. Their villages were also renamed in Spanish. Over time, Native traditions, ceremonies, and ways of dress were eliminated.

Bribes and Ceremonies

When a **friar** made his first contact with a Florida village, he tried to impress the villagers. He wore fancy clothes and used music, incense, candles, and sacred statues in his **rituals**. The friars focused on the chiefs: they knew if a chief converted, he would order his people to do so. The chiefs were given beads, clothing, and tools, and they often felt obliged to convert once they had accepted such gifts.

Most Native converts, however, simply added Christian practices to their own spiritual beliefs.

When they converted, chiefs had to pledge obedience to the Spanish king. Part of their pledge was that they would supply workers for the Spanish. Native people worked as laborers, planting crops, hauling supplies, and performing other menial tasks. Native people resented their slavery and sometimes **rebelled**. Spanish missionaries and soldiers dealt with rebels severely.

Decline of the Mission System

In 1655, there were 70 friars in Florida and about 40 missions. By 1680, however, the number of converts living in missions had fallen to 6,550 from a peak of 30,000 in 1635. The decline was mostly due to death from European diseases, but many people had been killed by soldiers also. Others moved to lands outside Spanish control. By 1700, the mission system was nearly gone.

Slave Labor

"For lack of pack animals, the said Indians bring on their back and transport the fruits and goods of the land. . . . [Many refuse to be Christians] in order not to experience similar labor, from which it has resulted in some dying on the roads . . ."

Royal Treasurer Don Joseph de Prado, writing to the governor of Florida about Native converts, 1654

Sometimes, Native people rebelled against the missions and missionaries. In this picture, men from different Florida villages unite for a battle against European colonists.

Conclusion

Florida Under Many Flags

By the 1600s, there were other Europeans colonizing parts of North America. In 1763, the British gained control of Florida. In 1783, after Britain's surrender to the United States at the end of the Revolutionary War in 1781, Spain got Florida back for a little while. In 1819, however, Spain gave Florida to the United States. The days of the Spanish Empire in North America were coming to an end.

The Seminole People

The Seminole people of Florida are the **descendants** of Creek Indians and also of Africans who escaped to Florida from slavery in the British colonies. After Florida became part of the United States, Americans tried to take Seminole land by force. The Seminoles resisted, and there were several wars between 1817 and 1858. Most Seminole people were forced to move to Oklahoma in the 1840s, but a few remained in southern Florida. They did not sign a peace treaty with the United States until 1935.

A group of Seminole people in traditional dress stand outside a thatched dwelling in the Florida Everglades in the 1930s.

Florida became a state in 1845. When the Civil War began in 1861, Florida joined the Confederate States of America, and so a fourth flag flew over the old fort at St. Augustine, now named Fort Marion. The town was reclaimed by the United States in 1862.

An International City

Over time, the city of St. Augustine became truly international. In addition to Native American, British, African, and Spanish people, there were settlers from Greece, Italy, Germany, France, and other countries. With so many cultures and nations represented, the people of St. Augustine had to learn how to get along with those who were different from themselves.

St. Augustine Today

In the 1880s, St. Augustine became a tourist resort. The town was busy with plays, concerts, dances, and sports. Beginning in the 1930s, the city government started restoring historic sites. Every year, thousands of tourists visit the living museum in the restored Spanish Quarter. The Castillo de San Marcos was restored to its original name in 1942, and it is now a national historic monument.

Flags in St. Augustine reflect its history. In the foreground is the British flag. and behind it the U.S. flag. Just visible is the Cross of Burgundy, used by Spain from the early 1500s until 1785.

27

Time Line

1513	April 2: Juan Ponce de León lands in Florida.
1564	French settlers build Fort Caroline in northern Florida.
1565	March 20: King Philip II of Spain authorizes Pedro Menéndez de Avilés to colonize Florida.
	September 8: Spanish colonists land and occupy Timucuan village of Seloy.
	September 20: Menéndez and his soldiers defeat French at Fort Caroline and capture fort.
1566	St. Augustine is rebuilt on Anastasia Island.
1572	St. Augustine is moved back to mainland and rebuilt.
1574	Pedro Menéndez dies.
1576	Native people attack and destroy Santa Elena and St. Augustine. Pedro Menéndez Marquez becomes governor of Florida.
1586	June 7–8: English fleet under Francis Drake attacks and burns St. Augustine.
1599	Fire and flooding destroy most of St. Augustine.
1671	Work begins on Castillo de San Marcos.
1763	Britain takes over Florida from Spain.
1783	Florida returns to Spanish rule.
1817	First Seminole War begins.
1819	Spain gives Florida to the United States.
1825	Castillo de San Marcos is renamed Fort Marion.
1835	Second Seminole War begins.
1845	Florida becomes a state.
1855	Third Seminole War begins.
1861	Florida joins the Confederate States of America.
1862	March 11: United States retakes St. Augustine.
1942	Fort Marion's name is restored to Castillo de San Marcos.

Things to Think About and Do

The Invaders Arrive

Imagine the life of a Timucuan person living in Florida in 1565, when the Spanish settlers arrive. Think about what happened and how they were treated. Now imagine the same thing happening in your town today. Suddenly, your home is no longer your own. People speaking a different language arrive with weapons superior to your own and demand you give up your land and way of life and become their slaves. Write about your experience, how it would feel, and what you would do in that situation.

Cultural Differences

When the Spanish arrived in Florida, they brought with them many foreign ideas and traditions. Find out about Spanish and Native life in the 1500s and list some of the differences. You could compare housing, food, spiritual beliefs, dress, weapons, entertainment, family life, and government.

Disasters in St. Augustine

St. Augustine suffered all kinds of disasters and attacks in its first 150 years. Imagine you are living in St. Augustine in the 1500s or 1600s during a flood, hurricane, fire, or attack by privateers or Timucuans. Write a journal for a day or two, describing the event.

Glossary

baptize:	make a person a Christian with a naming ceremony.
bastion:	stronghold or, in the case of the Castillo de San Marcos, part that sticks out of a fort or other stronghold.
colonist:	person who lives in a colony.
colony:	settlement, area, or country owned or controlled by another nation.
convert:	cause a person to change a belief, usually a religious one.
descendant:	person who comes in a later generation in a family. This could be a grandchild or someone many generations and years later.
empire:	political power controlling territory of colonies or other nations.
epidemic:	disease that spreads quickly and affects lots of people.
farrier:	person who shoes horses.
fleet:	group of ships under a single command.
friar:	man who belongs to a Catholic religious order.
garrison:	military post; also the troops stationed at a military post.
mission:	center built by the Spanish to convert Native Americans to Christianity and exploit their labor.
moat:	ditch surrounding fort or castle to protect it from intruders.
mortar:	type of cannon with a short barrel, used for firing shells.
natural resources:	naturally occurring materials, such as gold or wood, that can be used or sold.
privateer:	privately owned ship that attacks enemy ships; also a sailor who serves on such a ship.
rebel:	fight against a person or group in power.
ritual:	system of ceremonies in a religion.
sapling:	young tree small enough to have a thin, bendable trunk.
thatch:	dried grasses or leaves woven tightly together to make roofs.

Further Information

Books

Chui, Patricia and Jean Craven. *Florida: the Sunshine State* (World Almanac Library of the States). World Almanac Library, 2002.

Isaacs, Sally Senzell. *Life in St. Augustine* (Picture the Past). Heinemann Library, 2002.

Shuke, Heather. *The Timucua Indians: A Native American Detective Story* (Young Readers' Library). University Press of Florida, 2000.

Sita, Lisa. *Indians of the Northeast: Traditions, History, Legends, and Life* (Native Americans). Gareth Stevens, 2000.

Web Sites

www.ancientnative.org Heritage of the Ancient Ones, an organization devoted to preserving the history of Florida's Native people, offers lots of information about the Timucua and other groups.

www.flmnh.ufl.edu Florida Museum of Natural History has online exhibition that traces St. Augustine's history through archaeological finds.

www.nps/gov/casa Information about and pictures of the Castillo de San Marcos from the National Park Service, with good links to the web sites of other historical places in Florida.

Useful Addresses

Castillo de San Marcos National Monument
National Park Service
1 Castillo Drive East
St. Augustine, FL 32084
Telephone: (904) 829-6506

Index